The Never-Ending

POETRY BY ANDREW HUDGINS

Saints and Strangers (1985)
  with an introduction by John Frederick Nims

After the Lost War: A Narrative (1988)

The Never-Ending: New Poems (1991)

The Never-Ending

NEW POEMS BY

Andrew Hudgins

HOUGHTON MIFFLIN COMPANY

Boston   New York   London

Copyright © 1991 by Andrew Hudgins

For information about permission to reproduce selections from
this book, write to Permissions, Houghton Mifflin Company,
215 Park Avenue South, New York, New York 10003.

Library of Congress Cataloging-in-Publication Data

Hudgins, Andrew.
    The never-ending : new poems / by Andrew Hudgins.
        p.   cm.
    ISBN 0-395-58570-8   ISBN 0-395-58569-4 (pbk.)
    I. Title.
    PS3558.U288N48   1991   90-28173
    811 .54— dc20   CIP

Printed in the United States of America

BP   10   9   8   7   6   5   4   3   2   1

For Erin

If anyone asks you "what that is, of which the inherence makes the body hot," you will reply not heat (this is what I call the safe and stupid answer), but fire, a far superior answer.

— SOCRATES

Acknowledgments

Grateful acknowledgment is made to the following journals, in which some of the poems here were first published: *The Atlantic*: "In the Game"; *Crazyhorse*: "Rebuilding a Bird"; *The Georgia Review*: "How Shall We Sing the Lord's Song in a Strange Land?," "Heat Lightning in a Time of Drought"; *The Hudson Review*: "Green Inside the Door," "Two Worlds," "Fruit," "Bewilderments of the Eye," "Hunting with My Brother," "The Cestello Annunciation," "The Yellow Harvest," "New Headstones at the Shelby Springs Confederate Cemetery"; *Image*: "Lamentation over the Dead Christ"; *The Indiana Review*: "Hot August Nights"; *The Iowa Review*: "The Liar's Psalm," "The Unpromised Land"; *The Kenyon Review*: "Cargo," "Elegy for My Father, Who Is Not Dead"; *The Missouri Review*: "Psalm Against Psalms"; *The New Criterion*: "Raking Out the Nest," "Prayer for an Ex-Wife"; *The New England Review*: "Communion in the Asylum," "Praying Drunk"; *The New Republic*: "Crucifixion," "An Old Joke," "Beneath Searchlights," "Dead Christ"; *The New Virginia Review*: "The Gift"; *The Paris Review*: "As a Child in the Temple," "Mostly My Nightmares Are Dull," "Suffer the Children"; *Poetry*: "Compost: An Ode," "November Garden"; *Shenandoah*: "Two Ember Days in Alabama"; *The Southern Review*: "Against Gardens," "The Garden Changes," "The Ugly Flowers."

I'd like to express my deep appreciation to Princeton University. In 1989–90 I held the Alfred Hodder Fellowship at Princeton, which enabled me to finish this book. I'm grateful to the Taft Foundation at the University of Cincinnati for a summer grant that allowed me time to write, and to the Ohio Arts Council for an Individual Artist Fellowship. Thanks also to Walt Litz and Mike Kowalewski for their support. For detailed and honest

criticism of early versions of these poems, I owe a special debt
of gratitude to Peter Davison, Christianne Balk, and Richard
Selzer. "The Cestello Annunciation" is dedicated to Richard Sel-
zer and "The Gift" to Eric and Abby Walker.

Contents

The Never-Ending

How Shall We Sing the Lord's Song in a Strange Land?

We crept up, watched a black
man shovel dry bursts of dirt
into the air. Engrossed,
he didn't see me till
my friend hawked hard and then
stepped out of sight. The man
jerked back, convinced I'd come
to spit on him. Held there
by guilt that wasn't fairly mine,
I braced for what he'd say.
Instead, he smiled, forgave
the sin I hadn't sinned,
and turned back to his work.
I stumbled off and yelled,
Goddamn you! at my friend,
who laughed. Behind us, sand
exploded from the hole, caught wind,
and drifted slowly down
past headstones. Within a month
two boys found the black man hanging
from a hickory, his face
vague in a mist of gnats.
And every time they told the story
the gnats grew thicker, fiercer.
But I believed. I ached
the guiltless ache of dreams
and shuddered. A family that
I never saw mourned him.
Their lives changed and that change
spread out past my small-boy
imagining — though I
tried hard to follow it,

at twelve already remembering
how, ten years old, I'd stand
before the mirror and aim
a flashlight in my mouth.
White cheeks glowed red. I knew
that when I flicked the switch
I would no longer shine
with bloodlight, like stained glass.
I would return to the flesh
I'd always been. Back then,
I thought that if I could
I'd forgive nothing — I'd
change everything. But that's
before I learned how we
get trapped inside the haunts
and habits of this world.
While we drink coffee, gossip,
my cousin's daughter pounds on
the piano. It drives me nuts.
But Ellen's used to it.
The child plays till she drops,
and then we lug her
— elongated and limp — to bed.
My cousin tucks her in,
chooses one music box
from dozens on a shelf, winds it,
and sets it by her child's
damp head. The girl hums, drifts
from one world she creates
into another. A dark
circle of drool surrounds her head.
My cousin loves her with

the tenderness we save
for something that will ruin
our lives, break us, nail
us irretrievably
into this world, which we,
like good philosophers,
had meant to hate. This world,
this world is home. But it
will never feel like home.

The Cestello Annunciation

The angel has already said, *Be not afraid.*
He's said, *The power of the Most High*
will darken you. Her eyes are downcast and half closed.
And there's a long pause — a pause here of forever —
as the angel crowds her. She backs away,
her left side pressed against the picture frame.

He kneels. He's come in all unearthly innocence
to tell her of glory — not knowing, not remembering
how terrible it is. And Botticelli
gives her eternity to turn, look out the doorway, where
on a far hill floats a castle, and halfway across
the river toward it juts a bridge, not completed —

and neither is the touch, angel to virgin,
both her hands held up, both elegant, one raised
as if to say *stop*, while the other hand, the right one,
reaches toward his; and, as it does, it parts her blue robe
and reveals the concealed red of her inner garment
to the red tiles of the floor and the red folds

of the angel's robe. But her whole body pulls away.
Only her head, already haloed, bows,
acquiescing. And though she will, she's not yet said,
Behold, I am the handmaid of the Lord,
as Botticelli, in his great pity,

lets her refuse, accept, refuse, and think again.

Green Inside the Door

The summer we lived halfway underground
we watched legs scissor past, until the damp
grass grew to fill our window — wavering,
translucent with green light. Between snarled gibes
about some guy you'd kissed, how poor we were, the rain,
we sat on the couch silently and stared
into the wettest spring I've ever seen.
Warm water seeped through the walls and drenched the carpet.
We pulled it up and found another world
had thrived in darkness beneath our feet. It spread.
Exquisite variants of green ran riot,
dappling the walls with almost turquoise spores.
On top of them, starbursts
of black-green blossomed, blackened utter black —
as if mortality crept in each night
and pressed black kisses on the paint.
We scrubbed, waited a night, and they returned.
In bed, not touching, we dreamed they covered us.

At last, we stripped the whole place empty, tossed
shoes, chairs, and knickknacks on the lawn. Our yelling
frightened the neighbors and, hell, it scared us too.
Our red hands smoldered underneath harsh soap.
We fought, and scrubbed possessions till they broke
against the bristles. We left wet shattered things
out drying in the sun, returned
to almost barren rooms that reeked of bleach,
and slept still holding hands, raw burning hands
that we would not let go. Some books, some chairs,
some knickknacks all survived,
and so did we, my love, but separately.

Two Worlds

The bubble shuddering above my hand
mirrors, distorted on its skin, the world.
Dark pines bend inward on the sphere, and stars
bunch tightly in an arc across the curved
diminished night, lit by an oval moon.

It hits my hand, bounces, and in midbounce —
a graininess. The sphere dissolves. Thin drops
quiver in air, then fall across my palm.
The small night flies into the larger night,
where sweep from star to star seems firmly spaced,
one sun behind the next, a billion miles
from where I stand, my palm damp with the world
I held, however small or misshaped, on my hand.

Dead Christ

There seems no reason he should've died. His hands
are pierced by holes too tidy to have held,
untorn, hard muscles as they writhed on spikes.
And on the pink, scrubbed bottom of each foot
a bee-stung lip pouts daintily.
No reason he should die — and yet, and yet
Christ's eyes are swollen with it, his mouth
hangs slack with it, his belly taut with it,
his long hair lank with it, and damp;
and underneath the clinging funeral cloth
his manhood's huge and useless with it: Death.

One blood-drop trickles toward his wrist. Somehow
the grieving women missed it when they bathed,
today, the empty corpse. Most Christs return.
But this one's flesh. He isn't coming back.

The Ugly Flowers

The brown fields freeze, unfreeze.
Because there's little else
to love in March, I love
the ugly flowers — coarse,
unlovely things that stink:
wild ginger, skunk cabbage,
and stinking benjamin.
Though rank as rotten meat
and though they mimic spring-
thawed carcasses, they bloom
first — even if they bloom
the purple-brown of carrion.
That's what it takes to blossom
when earth thaws soft one day
and freezes hard the next.
But they don't hold our love.
Next come — still earlier
even than the bees — coltsfoot
and dandelion before
narcissus, daffodil,
and jonquil rise and dazzle us
like perfect Christs at Easter —
each one returned from death,
untouched by it, in glory.
And who remembers then
wild ginger, skunk cabbage,
and stinking benjamin,
and how we loved them when
they bloomed amid brown grass,
churned mud — the unloved loved,
the death-plant beautiful.

Hot August Nights

The men downstairs are making love.
With all the oohs and yelps, it sounds
a little like the ambulances that whoop
along the highway, then accelerate
toward Baptist Hospital. At night
the sirens moan and throb like passion —
or so it seems as I lie in my bed,
no breeze, the thick air wet and sticky.
From ten P.M. till three, the horns
race through the sweat-soaked night: race out,
return with bodies, their long moans
sometimes in rising harmony
with my loud neighbors down below,
who are so young they seem as if
they never stop, hold back, delay
their celebrations of the night:
touch, hold, let go — each body stunned
against the fierce want of the other.
But they will age, grow colder. They might
break up and fight till someone's hurt.
Perhaps they'll need an ambulance.
Hot nights incline me to these thoughts,
despairs. At other times, in winter,
I have no interest in the night,
the things that happen there, when sirens
sing with yet another tragedy
or accident. It wears me out.
And who can dwell too much on pain
when it is someone else's and
I'm warm, drowsy, almost asleep,
lulled by the murmuring downstairs?
But when I wake, the morning news

tells of a man who killed himself
with thirty-seven hammer blows
upside the head. Perhaps last night
his sirens lulled me off to sleep.
I've come to count on them. At times,
when there was someone here with me,
the sirens kept her up, and tense,
because she wasn't used to them.
And I tried to explain: *They're lullabies,*
they sound like making love. She looked
carefully at me, decided that I lacked
some fundamental sympathy,
so I tried harder to describe
the harsh, accelerating cries,
the easing off, the murmuring.
Dear God, it's just this heat, and what
I tell myself so I can sleep
when, after midnight, I hear sirens.

Lamentation over the Dead Christ

Dismiss the body bent so awkwardly
across his mother's lap: there's no god in it.
Dismiss the saint holding the nails, the thorns.
Remember only Marys: Salome,
Cleophas, Magdalene —
and Mary, fainted virgin, her body huge,
distended, bulging, because she suffers more
than anyone can grieve until she loosens
her human shape, becomes impossible.
And Saint John's arm elongates eerily
because he cannot comfort her or ease
her body back to what it was.
The other Marys, too, contort. Their muscles
twist and their bodies bend
until they're radiant with suffering.

And though she wouldn't want you to,
remember Magdalene. She's hunchbacked, wrenched
by dark, misshaping sorrow.
Her first eyes glittered with hatred, rage.
But in her grief she cried to Botticelli,
Erase my eyes! Instead, he's hidden them
behind two raw, enormous hands. She'd begged,
and Botticelli, unlike God, said *yes.*

Beneath Searchlights

Shop windows glow like fish tanks. Even in town
the sky's so full of stars I can imagine
sun beyond sun until there seems no darkness
in the dark — a trick the mind plays against midnight.
But just a trick. It doesn't change the darkness:
cats yowl, my dog's hair bristles in response.
He's snuffling at a bush when suddenly
harsh light explodes around me. And then I hear
the *whup, whup, whup* of helicopter blades
above and slightly to the left — the spot,
though higher, where I imagine my soul drifts
and watches me. The searchlight lingers.
The taut leash makes my hand point toward the dog.
Come here, I hiss. He's busy. I haul him, choking,
into the light. Now that my alibi
stands growling at my side, I dance a jig,
then bow — but upward, blindly. As if applauding,
the spotlight dips once, veers off, scraping hard
light over houses, trees. The choked dog whimpers.
He jerks, I pull, and we compose one linked
uneasy beast that seesaws through dark streets,
this way and that, toward home, sleep, food, and work —
repeat, repeat, repeat until we die.
But that's untrue. Too stark. Sometimes — tonight —
I satisfy the light that questions me.

An Old Joke

They'd rushed so close to her, their stones
were pelting one another. Christ
pushed roughly through the crowd and shouted,
Let him without sin cast the next stone.
The crowd paused, thinking. Then out of nowhere,
out of the shuffling, silenced crowd,
one stone flew, hit the woman. She dies.
And in the joke I started out to tell,
Christ looks into the crowd and howls,
Goddammit, Mother — that's not funny!

But I have sinned enough to understand
it wasn't she, not Mary. It was the man
who still had love's scent on his flesh,
love's fragrance on his hands, as he selected
one stone, weighed it, thought twice, three times,
then threw — and baffled Christ, who thought
it was his perfect mother, correcting him.

Praying Drunk

Our Father who art in heaven, I am drunk.
Again. Red wine. For which I offer thanks.
I ought to start with praise, but praise
comes hard to me. I stutter. Did I tell you
about the woman whom I taught, in bed,
this prayer? It starts with praise; the simple form
keeps things in order. I hear from her sometimes.
Do you? And after love, when I was hungry,
I said, *Make me something to eat.* She yelled,
Poof! You're a casserole! — and laughed so hard
she fell out of the bed. Take care of her.

Next, confession — the dreary part. At night
deer drift from the dark woods and eat my garden.
They're like enormous rats on stilts except,
of course, they're beautiful. But why? What *makes*
them beautiful? I haven't shot one yet.
I might. When I was twelve, I'd ride my bike
out to the dump and shoot the rats. It's hard
to kill your rats, our Father. You have to use
a hollow point and hit them solidly.
A leg is not enough. The rat won't pause.
Yeep! Yeep! it screams, and scrabbles, three-legged, back
into the trash, and I would feel a little bad
to kill something that wants to live
more savagely than I do, even if
it's just a rat. My garden's vanishing.
Perhaps I'll merely plant more beans, though that
might mean more beautiful and hungry deer.
Who knows?
           I'm sorry for the times I've driven
home past a black, enormous, twilight ridge.

Crested with mist, it looked like a giant wave
about to break and sweep across the valley,
and in my loneliness and fear I've thought,
O let it come and wash the whole world clean.
Forgive me. This is my favorite sin: despair —
whose love I celebrate with wine and prayer.

Our Father, thank you for all the birds and trees,
that nature stuff. I'm grateful for good health,
food, air, some laughs, and all the other things
I'm grateful that I've never had to do
without. I have confused myself. I'm glad
there's not a rattrap large enough for deer.
While at the zoo last week, I sat and wept
when I saw one elephant insert his trunk
into another's ass, pull out a lump,
and whip it back and forth impatiently
to free the goodies hidden in the lump.
I could have let it mean most anything,
but I was stunned again at just how little
we ask for in our lives. *Don't look! Don't look!*
Two young nuns tried to herd their giggling
schoolkids away. *Line up,* they called. *Let's go
and watch the monkeys in the monkey house.*
I laughed, and got a dirty look. Dear Lord,
we lurch from metaphor to metaphor,
which is — let it be so — a form of praying.

I'm usually asleep by now — the time
for supplication. Requests. As if I'd stayed
up late and called the radio and asked
they play a sentimental song. Embarrassed.

I want a lot of money and a woman.
And, also, I want vanishing cream. You know —
a character like Popeye rubs it on
and disappears. Although you see right through him,
he's there. He chuckles, stumbles into things,
and smoke that's clearly visible escapes
from his invisible pipe. It makes me think,
sometimes, of you. What makes me think of me
is the poor jerk who wanders out on air
and then looks down. Below his feet, he sees
eternity, and suddenly his shoes
no longer work on nothingness, and down
he goes. As I fall past, remember me.

Fruit

Each fall I prune the fig or it'll choke
with growth. The suckers shoot in every gap
or lunge into the sky. With lopping shears
I cut them flush against the limb, amazed
what steel and leverage will do to wood.
I prune to make the tree more logical,
a crazy thought. A fig tree wants to fill
the world with leaves. But I want fruit. I cut,
go slow, study, applying logic where
its ruthlessness will not be loved till spring
when almost shapeless gobs of seed and sugar
will fall apart, melt on my tongue like jam.
I oil the pruning shears, put them away,
and leave the tree alone to do its work.

Bewilderments of the Eye

The bewilderments of the eye are of two kinds
and arise from two causes, either from coming out
of the light or going into the light.

— PLATO

My neighbor's bug light sizzles beyond the hedge
until I want to scream. A loud, wild shriek
would serve the bastard right for all the death
he's meting out. Oh, sure, it's only bugs,
but when you're down you pity even them.
My self-indulgent soul leads me to pray,
God bless the moth, whose nervous system just
says *light, light, light, light, light* — the thing it loves.
I've learned to gauge the noise and estimate
what bug is zapped. Large ones fight back. Mosquitoes
disintegrate in one electric snap.

The thin, sweet smell of Malathion drifts
over the hedge. Some folks can't take the world,
its flaws. My neighbor's one and so am I,
although I lack his energy. Young swifts,
attracted by the bugs, have fallen in
the blue current. Sometimes they make it out.
It's fifty-fifty live or die, I'd guess.

Idly, I slap mosquitoes as they land,
and if they leave a spot of blood, it's shared:
once mine, then theirs, now mine again. The moths,
when I go in and douse the light, possess
no purpose in their lives, not even death,

beating into the darkness and the trees,
where they don't want to fly — as once, sleepless,
I stood right here and watched the opposite:
two barn owls flying hard across the dawn,
no longer hunting, hurrying toward darkness,
paler, paler, till they disappeared
in the failure of my eyes in too much light.

Two Ember Days in Alabama

I.

Out with my dog at dawn — we couldn't sleep —
I met a woman hanging laundry, mist
rising from warm, wet clothes. The empty forms
flapped on the line like pieces of three ghosts
filling with wind before they froze. And further on,
in woods, I saw the vaguely hourglass shape
my boot had stamped in mud the day before,
and, frozen in it, the hoofprint of a deer.
Dan sniffed it, whined, jerked at the leash, his nose
aimed low into the brambled underbrush.
We circled home past bright clothes frozen stiff.
Like pendulums, they ticktocked in the wind.

I shivered underneath cold, rumpled sheets
and so did Dan, who warmed my feet. At noon
we didn't budge. Rain, like a gray hammer, fell.
By now my footprints and the deer's have merged
in mud, the wild spring loosening of earth.

2.

My tomcats saunter from near woods, and when
I hold them, resisting, up against my cheek
I smell — what is it? Smoke, confused with fur.
And now, in deepest Lent, an Ember Day,
I marvel at the inconclusive whiff of fire
that lingers there. This Lent, too, lingers on
like twilight or the study of last things.
The blackbirds peck through dried-up winter weeds.
There's nothing much to eat that I can see,
but they are fat and glossy as eight balls.
As I walk out the door, they rise and join
the northward stream of blackbirds, grackles, crows
that have for days been building energy
for exodus. They've swelled the barren woods,
loading the unleaved trees like the black fruit
of nothingness. And now they simply leave.
First fall, then winter. Then this long pause. And then
the starting over. And then the never-ending.

Heat Lightning in a Time of Drought

My neighbor, drunk, stood on his lawn and yelled,
Want some! Want some! He bellowed it as cops
cuffed him, shoved him in their back seat — *Want some!* —
and drove away. Now I lie here awake,
not by choice, listening to the crickets' high
electric trill, urgent with lust. Heat lightning flashes.
The crickets will not, will not stop. I wish
that I could shut the window, pull the curtain, sleep.
But it's too hot. *Want some!* He screamed it till
I was afraid I'd made him up to scream
what I knew better than to say out loud
although it's August-hot and every move
bathes me in sweat and we are careless,
careless, careless, every one of us,
and when my neighbor screams out in his yard
like one dog howling for another dog,
I call the cops, then lie in my own sweat,
remembering the woman
who, at a party on a night this hot,
walked up to me, propped her chin on my chest,
and sighed. She was a little drunk, the love-light
unshielded in her eyes. We fell in love.
One day at supper the light fixture dropped,
exploded on the table. Glass flew around us,
a low, slow-motion blossoming of razors.
She was unhurt till I reached out my hand
— left hand — to brush glass from her face.
Two drops of blood ran down her cheek.
On TV, I'd seen a teacher dip a rose
in liquid nitrogen. When he withdrew it,
it smoked, frozen solid. He snapped one petal, frail
as isinglass, and then, against the table,

he shattered it. The whole rose blew apart.
Like us. And then one day the doorbell rang.
A salesman said, *Watch this!* He stripped my bed
and vacuumed it. The nozzle sucked up two
full, measured cups of light gray flakes. He said,
That's human skin. I stood, refusing the purchase,
stood staring at her flesh and mine commingled
inside the measuring cup, stood there and thought,
*She's been gone two years, she's married, and all this time
her flesh has been in bed with me.* Don't laugh.
Don't laugh. That's what the Little Moron says
when he arrives home early from a trip
and finds his wife in bed with someone else.
The man runs off. The Little Moron puts
a pistol to his own head, cocks the hammer.
His wife, in bed, sheets pulled up to her breasts,
starts laughing. *Don't you laugh!* he screams. *Don't laugh —
you're next.* It is the wisest joke I know because
the heart's a violent muscle, opening
and closing. Who knows what we might do:
by night, the craziness of dreams; by day,
the craziness of logic. Listen!
My brother told me of a man wheeled, screaming,
into the ward, a large Coke bottle rammed
up his ass. I was awed: there is no telling
what we'll do in our fierce drive to come together.
The heart keeps opening and closing like a mine
where fire still burns, a century underground,
following the veins of black coal, rearing up
to take a barn, a house, a pasture. Although
I wish that it would rain tonight, I fret
about the heat lightning that flicks and glitters

on the horizon as if it promised rain.
It can't. But I walk outside, stand on parched grass,
and watch it hungrily — all light, all dazzle —
remembering how we'd drive out past the town's light,
sit on the hood, and watch great thunderheads
huge as a state — say, Delaware — sail past. Branched
lightning jagged, burst the dark from zenith to horizon.
We stared at almost nothing: some live oaks,
the waist-high corn. Slow raindrops smacked the corn,
plopped in the dirt around us, drummed the roof,
and finally reached out, tapped us on the shoulders.
We drove home in the downpour, laughed, made love
— still wet with rain — and slept. But why stop there?
Each happy memory leads me to a sad one:
the friend who helped me through my grief by drinking
all of my liquor. And when, at last, we reached
the wretched mescal, he carefully sliced off
the worm's black face, ate its white body, staggered
onto this very lawn, and racked and heaved
until I helped him up. *You're okay, John.*
You've puked it out. "No, man — you're wrong. That worm
ain't ever coming out." Heat lightning flashes.
No rain falls and no thunder cracks the heat.
No first concussion dwindles to a long
low rolling growl. I go in the house, lie down,
pray, masturbate, drift to the edge of sleep.
I wish my soul were larger than it is.

The Yellow Harvest

After last harvest, as the trees blaze orange,
three peasant women trudge
through stubble fields and kneel, heads bowed,
before the yellow Christ. On their stripped field,

Gauguin has painted his last cross
and nailed himself to it. Gauguin:
there's no mistaking that thin beard, that face,
that tilt of head. But he's no longer Paul Gauguin.

Bright yellow tinged with green — the color
of the autumn fields stretched out behind him —
he's Christ. He's harvested: cut, bundled,
and, like a last shock of late wheat,

left in the field past gathering.
And this Christ knows he's dying. He yearns
to return — to bloom, seed, wither, die,
and come again. The women gathered at his feet

pray to endure the winter, pray
to eat, keep warm, and prosper. But Christ,
who was once Paul Gauguin,
sags on his cross. The yellow hills,

the yellow valley, and the gleaned
dry yellow hills — all dying — call,
O Son of Man, we're coming back.
Put down your soul and follow us.

The Liar's Psalm

He that cannot wimple false hood in truth's kerchief,
hath neither art nor cunning; but he that can do it,
and deliver error without stammering, he may do wonders,
he may wear scarlet, gray, and purple . . . But to speak
truth is no cunning, it never makes the evil one laugh.
To lie well and with grace; to lift up wrong above right;
to make mountains and build castles in the air; to make
men juggle and look through their fingers, and all for the
hope of gain only: this, nephew, is an art beyond expression;
yet evermore of the end cometh misery and affliction.

— REYNARD THE FOX

I. HOMAGE TO THE FOX

Let us make homage to the fox, for his tail is as lush
as Babylon. His eyes, all glitter and distrust,
are cruel as a Spanish crucifixion, and his paws so subtle
they can empty your refrigerator without the light
coming on. But these virtues
aren't why we praise the fox. Let us make homage
for he's a liar nonpareil and there is none as ruthless.
His gorgeous tongue is more lush than
his tail, sharper than his eyes, quicker than his paws.
Magnificent instrument! Equal parts oil and sugar, grease
     and candy,
and there is no truth in it — praise the fox. Everything
is intricately
untrue, Byzantine, consistent unto its own rules, easier said
than done, because there are lies ad infinitum and one truth,
     and that

monk-drab to him who wears sport coats by Calder
and iridescent pants. His tongue is honed on glass. The rabbit
he shreds like confetti and the feathers of the duck
are pasted to his grin, which is tighter
than Torquemada's and would make opposing counsel weep.
The fox — praise him in parts and praise him whole — makes
    no
bones about it. The truth is lack of courage,
failure of imagination, low stakes, high dudgeon, middle
    passage,
and there is no profit in it. Praise him for deceit.
We have business to conduct with him and we don't stand
    a chance.
Praise him. His tongue will cleanse our bones. Praise the fox.

2. REPENTANCE

I repent the actual. It has never got me anywhere.
It is nothing against principalities, against powers.
My father will die and I will carry on. I dread his death

more than mine because it will come sooner — knowledge
    I repent. In lies
he will outlive the liar. And that's me. The lie itself
will carry on, is itself a child, a separate life, a blow

against the gods of objects. Who are not happy with me
or with their densities. They are not worth their flawed
    kingdoms.
And neither do I love them. They are dangerous. They are too

stupid to be insignificant, too proud of their ability
to blister my hands and make them raw. I repent letting them,
and I repent logic, which has no god: it will do

anything, it will go anywhere. Tell it your destination
and it will take you there. A taxi. *This* is the nature
of evidence: how could you prove the meat you ate last night

wasn't horse meat, goat flesh,
or something I had, the night before, sliced from my thighs?
Or that it was meat at all? Or that you ate? There is no

bottom to what we will believe, and no top.
So I have made this vow.
Never again will I insult you with the actual, something

that has no birthday, while lies are born
six times a second and each with a festival. They are the gifts
we give ourselves, like morphine, a change of clothes, a piece

of apple pie, a black chrysanthemum, a job — I could go on.
I am ashamed when I remember whom I have attacked
with actuality. My mother with her stinginess. My wife

with her black and purple dress — you should have seen it! —
and her infidelities. My friend who steals ashtrays. My
    brother's
avoirdupois. I repent that blade and I repent

my skill with it. When blessed with falsehoods, I will tell them.
When told a lie, I will believe it. I will not doubt
a word you say. Forgive me now my finger in the wound, and
    knuckle deep.

3. JUDAS, FLOWERING

Everybody has a hero. He is mine. Who would I be
if I hadn't polished evil like a pair of shoes
and walked across my life in them? And though
I've long since worn the bottoms through, the tops
are bright as bulbs. They light my path. Without them I would
    be barred
from restaurants. But, Judas, do I have to be quite
so human in my brilliant shoes? I'm not complaining. Lies are
    enough.
They are the grease that slips a camel through
the needle's eye. He doesn't even have to touch the sides
unless I say he does. Thank you. And lies
are just a start. The world is rich
with penny-ante lies and frugal sins. Since I am wrong
I want to do it right. I want to be spectacularly wrong
so I may, in the crowd, be noticed, lifted out, preserved,
redeemed. I need the big betrayal, the perfidy
that Botticelli knew but didn't understand. In *Calumny*
a prince has protracted, pointed, velvet donkey ears, and to
    those ears
— those gorgeous ass's ears! — cling Ignorance
and Suspicion. They love those wonderful ears! And there
    is Calumny,
her fingers laced into the hair of a man
she's dragged before the prince. His hands are locked
in prayer. Why bother? She is beautiful and the prince has
    ass's ears.
Last, late, and hardly interesting at all
is Veritas. I stare at her
as reverent as Satan staring at the face of Eve.

4. APPEAL TO THE WHIRLWIND

Give me the gifts: love, hope, and treachery —
these three. But treachery has the great claim: complication.
Formal and elaborate, aching to be

slapped down, it opens doors in asphalt, makes something
out of nothing — out of nothing at all.
In blank unpredatory sky it sees a goshawk blurred

in the radical of its descent. The point at which it strikes meat
is Archimedean. Done poorly, treachery can budge the world.
  I want
to do it well. I want to be the missionary who refuses,

point blank, to mention grace to natives — even
when they ask. He won't be drawn out. He lets their souls
  — the souls of head-hunters and cannibals! — languish

and find their own way to perdition. When they press him,
he puts his finger in his mouth and cocks his thumb.
That too is a lie. Treachery is taut between the world and us,

and it is useful in the prevention of disease. It drops us down
into risk, down into percentages and decimal points. It denies
    death
and makes our lives worthwhile. I told a friend, *The moon*

is only part of it. Once we get evening hacked away
the whole night sky will look like that. She didn't buy a word
    I said,
but still she held my hand between her knees as we drove

into a plum-colored dusk too beautiful to see. We skipped joy
and went right to the crying, the gnashing of teeth. We
    were very
good at it. We will improve. I trust the suffering —

like bone in flesh, it will endure. Still, what I said
about the moon is something I believe. A gift
the liar gives himself, like carelessness or truth.

Rebuilding a Bird

dreaming of Audubon

The ape stared at the bird, then pulled
the cage onto his lap. His loose
hands dipped between the bars and cupped
both wings against the bird's green body.
The parrot shrieked *hellow* and fought.
Struck motionless, I watched. The wings
came free and in that coming free
I saw how living flesh could be
dismantled. The red machinery
of meat — joint, muscle, bone — is there,
below, as real as what's on top.
I saw how deep you have to go
to get the surface right. I yelled.
The monkey looked at me, and then
reached up and twisted off her head.
I've spent most of my life since then
rebuilding birds. You slide the scalpel
between the joints, you separate
tough sinews from frail bones, you probe
recesses of the viscera,
and spread the parts across your table.
Sometimes it takes three tanagers
to rebuild one. And with those parts
I build it up again with wire,
sawdust, and glue. I make it look
as if it flew through death untouched
and out the other side. Such nonsense!
I've left science and moved to art,
where sins persisted in enough
may lead to grace. And if I climbed
a live oak, sailed the remade bird,

it would skitter through bright oak leaves,
smack ground, and break, becoming ugly —
and looks are all it has, once flight
has been dissected from its wings.
But my art has its moments too.
It's never far from awe, which is
a sort of holy ignorance
that thrives on surfaces, grows rich
on facts as it moves down, like knives,
through deeper, stranger surfaces.
Once you've dismantled cardinals
the ones you see break from a larch
and skim, undulant, across the pond
are never quite the same. They're sparks
thrown off by their own inner fire,
but even more mysterious
than fire. I study their red flicker,
thrilled and regretful, as the gun
rests on my forearm. The screeching monkey voice
of a pileated woodpecker will,
at times, freeze my cheek on the gunstock
as if I'd heard my own soul speak
inside the wild leaves of an oak. I'm glad
to let its mocking voice escape,
though it's the one I want to catch
and hold, someday, beneath the knife.

The Gift

They hung the lambs and cut their white throats. Blood
flowed down their chins and into earthen bowls.
Each time one filled, another bowl was placed
beneath the stream. Inside the pit, mesquite
burned down to an orange pulse, a coat of ash.

You asked about their myths and now, at last,
they talked as they prepared the feast. They stuffed
the carcasses with masa, then packed the hole
with four lambs, three full jars of blood. Green leaves
were tucked around the meat and everything
was buried. The dirt included excrement.

All night you hunkered on your heels, talked, smoked,
almost forgot the buried flesh because
they offered you a legend no one outside
had ever heard. The coals burned slowly. At dawn
they dug it up: the tainted meat, the jars
of hot, gelatinous blood. Already knowing
how it would double you with cramps and heaving,
you held the rough bowl in both hands, flinched once,
then drank, from courtesy, the ruinous cup,
almost eager now that you had no choice.

Christ Carrying the Cross

Two crosses on a hill await a third.
A crowd stands in a circle as other townsfolk
swarm slowly up the hill to join them. Where's Christ?
They frolic, gossip, rear their horses, laugh.
Even the soldiers celebrate. They sport
red jackets as they keep some order here.
Not too much. It's an execution, after all.
Where's Christ? There are the thieves. In a horse cart,
one prays, one stares into the sky and howls.
Where's Christ? There's a small town, there's a crag
with a black windmill, rickety, on top.
And there's Christ, hard to see, right in the center.
He's fallen beneath his huge cross. Can he rise?
The revelers kick and taunt him. At church we sing,
Were you there when they crucified my Lord?
A crow perched on a torture-wheel looks off
into the distance. Christ staggers, falls, stays down.
Eternity's a long walk, Lord. Get up!

In the Game

From deep left field, I watch the hitter.
Then, bored, I watch a hawk, tip feathers
adjusting as he hunts. Air jolts.
Flatcars jerk past. From underneath thick netting,
artillery splotched with camouflage
aims past our playing field. I turn
and gawk, awed by the huge green weapons,
as if I had forgotten somehow
the necessary violences
that let us play our game. Behind me
my brother yells, *Get in the game!*
It's late. I think we're two runs down.
Mike charges a weak grounder, whips
the ball to first. Out three, thank God.
As I jog across the parched infield,
the slow train churns the air
explosively and I remember when
Mike ran home from a ballgame, fell
on the front lawn, heatstruck, and thrashed
until I leapt across his chest. He yelled,
Don't let me hurt anybody! but a wild
blow clipped my cheek and, shit, I slammed
my fist, twice, hard — into his ribs.
We fought till Momma turned the hose on us.
Mike pushed himself free, walked, embarrassed,
into the house. He has, of course,
hurt others — as I, by telling this,
hurt him again to help myself
toward understanding, a vicious truth
and one I cannot do without
though I don't care to think about it,
like this slow military train

that jolts into the distance. Green, tan,
and olive splotches blend with pines,
invisible. I cannot tell
exactly where they merge, become
the same thing. Natural and unnatural —
I used to be so sure which one
was which. The umpire calls strike one
while I stand stupid, thinking. But then
I bear down, double to right. Mike tears
past third, slides hard, and sends the catcher sprawling.
He yells. Mike yells back, shoves. I edge off second,
judging the steal. We're one behind,
with one man, me, on base.

The Adoration of the Magi

A boy — okay, it's me — wears a fringed
blue tablecloth and fidgets as Joseph
in his church Christmas play. He watches
ten-year-old magi with false beards
hold out gold, frankincense, and myrrh.
Dear God, he's desperate to pee.
Six angels with coat-hanger wings
dance by. Their tinfoil halos tilt
and slide down on their foreheads. One,
too large, has fallen past a girl's
small nose and hangs about her neck.
She pulls it up, keeps dancing. He smirks.
And each time Mary lifts her child
its doll-eyes click open and then
clack shut when she lays Jesus down.
What's wrong with me? he thinks, despairing.
Why won't my soul expand with reverence?
He hopes no one can tell by looking at him.
The pressure in his loins makes him dizzy.
He sways. The Youth Choir warbles, *Hark,
the herald angels sing.* The curtain drops.
And that grim boy bolts off, stage left,
one hand pressed hard into his crotch.

Suffer the Children

The tail, held back along the spine, keeps them
— most times — from kicking you. I don't know why.
As Pa clamped down on the bull's sack, I dropped
the tail to watch. The bull lashed out and kicked
Pa backward through the door of his flimsy shed,
and Pa got up, picked up a four by four,
and with three blows drove that bull to its knees
and with two more blows drove it to the ground.
He finished clamping off the balls in silence,
drove to the doctor's house. Three broken ribs,
a ruptured spleen. He didn't yell at me.
He groaned each time the pickup truck hit a bump.
He screamed when nurses carried him inside.
But he never said a word to me, or told.

As a Child in the Temple

"I'm looking forward to my death," she said.
I sat upright. I watched her blond hair sway,
this college girl who taught our Sunday School.
"In death, we'll see God face to face," she said.
"Now through a glass darkly. Then, face to face."
She cried a tear or two, composed herself,
and said, "Let's turn our Bibles to First John . . ."

I didn't. "Hell," I whispered to a friend,
"if she's so hot to die, who's stopping her?"

But now I'm older than that girl, by far,
and she's become her wish to die, some tears,
and now, most vividly, that swaying length
of ash-blond hair — that hair, and my relief.
Not understanding meant I wasn't Christ.
I didn't have to love death. I was reprieved,
saved, not for the last time, by my ignorance.

Hunting with My Brother

My brother blasts pigeons beneath the bridge
and lets them lie. *They're only flying rats,*
he says, and just like Daddy I snap, "Two wrongs
don't make a right." *But two rights make a left,*
he says. We laugh, and talk of how his wife
cooks squirrels with dumplings and black pepper
and how my garden's gone to seed.

He swings the shotgun to his shoulder. Two quick
squirrels scrabble, spiraling up a water oak.
Frustrated, Mike fires into the ragged nests.
"Hey, knock it off!" I yell. He shrugs,
twists up the choke, and fires again.
I grab the barrel and wrench it. His fist
clips my left ear. I cock my fist.
But we're already backing off,
apologizing — unlike when, younger,
we'd roll across the ground, kick, gouge,
and bite.

We hike two miles in silence.
Mike's wife looks from the kitchen window.
We hold up empty hands and shrug. She laughs.
We glare at her and, goddamn, she laughs louder.
Then slowly we laugh too. Who wouldn't laugh
at Cain and Abel coming home —
no meat, no beans, and both alive.

November Garden

The zinnias — cut-and-come-again —
are dry as Mother's hair. They crush
beneath my hand. The lilies

are further gone than that, sunk down
into their bulbs, as Mother has
gone underground. Each spring they burst

into their almost human flesh —
white blooms like all they've ever made.
But not the same. A different bud

dyed with the same returning color.
The marigolds, though, cannot withdraw.
They're hybrids. They don't seed. Next year

they won't be back. And so they flower,
the withered blooms beside the red ones,
which now seem garish, tawdry, cheap.

I pluck the dry, brown clusters. The reds
bloom grimly through a dozen frosts
to the first hard freeze. They cannot stop.

Funeral Parlor Fan

Inside the Vineyard Baptist Church,
the funeral parlor fans — tick tock —
snapped hot air in the faces of
grandmother, mother, aunt. They kept
a steady out-of-sequence beat. Me, I faltered.
I'd lay the creased fan on my lap
and stare at Jesus kneeling in
Gethsemane. He didn't look
like someone pleading not to die.
If I were him I'd blubber worse
than when my daddy snapped his belt
out backward, popping through the loops,
tick tock. With a child's low cunning, I screamed
before the thin strap stung my thighs.
This Jesus didn't seem to get it: men
were going to drive three nails through him
and into wood and let him hang
there, writhing, till he died. I shuddered.
But I was eight and there were tons
of things I didn't get. I fanned
a little more, grew bored, elbowed my brother,
and kicked the pew in front of me,
till, casually, my mother's hand
dipped out and popped my head, not hard,
with Jesus praying in the garden
or, flipped, Hobb's Funeral Home. And just
to hear myself talk, I'd say *ouch*
and get another dose of Jesus,
and slightly harder too. The beat
resumed: tick tock, tick tock, and I
took up the worn, two-sided fan
and tried — small hands — to keep the beat.
Tick: Jesus. Tock: Hobb's Funeral Home.

Elegy for My Father, Who Is Not Dead

One day I'll lift the telephone
and be told my father's dead. He's ready.
In the sureness of his faith, he talks
about the world beyond this world
as though his reservations have
been made. I think he wants to go,
a little bit — a new desire
to travel building up, an itch
to see fresh worlds. Or older ones.
He thinks that when I follow him
he'll wrap me in his arms and laugh,
the way he did when I arrived
on earth. I do not think he's right.
He's ready. I am not. I can't
just say good-bye as cheerfully
as if he were embarking on a trip
to make my later trip go well.
I see myself on deck, convinced
his ship's gone down, while he's convinced
I'll see him standing on the dock
and waving, shouting, *Welcome back.*

Mostly My Nightmares Are Dull

Mostly my nightmares are dull. On autumn nights
I rake the yard. Brown leaves fall faster, faster.
They swamp my ankles, rise up past my knees,
waist, neck, until I'm drowning in dry leaves.
A bourgeois nightmare, sure. But still
I wake up sweaty, short of breath, surprised
at just how little fear it takes to break me.
And worse, some nights I raise the dead. I say,
I didn't understand that you were dying,
but Mother simply waves my guilt away,
left-handed, as though it were tobacco smoke.
Grandmother smiles, forgives my vulgar mouth,
and Sister, dead before my birth, confides
that she too loves Ray Charles. Soon Grandma's talk
of niggers makes me snarl at her. She sulks.
Her sulking makes me yell, Mom cries, Ray sings,
and Sister lapses back into her silence.
I wake, they die again, and I walk out
into a day I'll live as carelessly
as if I'll only — fat chance — live it once.

Ecce Homo

Christ bends, protects his groin. Thorns gouge
his forehead, and his legs
are stippled with dried blood. The part of us
that's Pilate says, *Behold the man.*
We glare at that bound, lashed,
and bloody part of us that's Christ. We laugh, we howl,
we shout, *Give us Barabbas,*
not knowing who Barabbas is, not caring.
A thief? We'll take him anyway. A drunk?
A murderer? Who cares? It's better him
than this pale, ravaged thing, this god. Bosch knows.
His humans waver, laugh, then change to demons
as if they're seized by epilepsy. It spreads
from eye to eye, from laugh to laugh until,
incited by the ease of going mad,
they go. How easy evil is! Dark voices sing,
You can be evil or you can be good,
but good is dull, my darlings, good is dull.
And we're convinced: How lovely evil is!
How lovely hell must be! *Give us Barabbas!*

Lord Pilate clears his throat and tries again:
I find no fault in this just man.
It's more than we can bear. In gothic script
our answer floats above our upturned eyes.
O crucify, we sing. *O crucify him!*

Compost: An Ode

Who can bring a clean thing
out of an unclean?

   — JOB 14:4

The beauty of the compost heap is not
the eye's delight.
                    Eyes see too much.
                                    They see
blood-colored worms
                    and bugs so white they seem
to feed off ghosts. Eyes
                    do not see the heat
that simmers in
                the moist heart of decay —
in its unmaking,
                making fire,
                        just hot
enough to burn
                itself. In summer, the heap
burns like a stove. It can — almost — hurt you.
I've held my hand inside the fire and counted
one, two, three,
                four.
                    I cannot hold it there.
Give it to me, the heat insists. *It's mine.*
I yank it back and wipe it on my jeans
as if
      I'd really heard the words.
                      And eyes
cannot appreciate
                sweet vegetable rot,

how good it smells
                    as everything dissolves,
dispersing
          back from thing
                         into idea.

From our own table we are feeding it
what we don't eat. Orange rind and apple core,
corn husks,
               and odds and ends the children smear
across their plates — we feed them all into the slow,
damp furnace of decay. Leaves curl at edges,
buckle,
          collapsing down into their centers,
as everything turns loose its living shape
and blackens, gives up
                       what it once was
to become dirt. The table scraps
and leafage join,
                  indistinguishable,
the way that death insists it's all the same,
while life
          must do a million things at once.
The compost heap is both — life, death — a slow
simmer,
          a leisurely collapsing of
the thing
          into its possibilities —
both bean and hollyhock, potato, zinnia, squash:
the opulence
             of everything that rots.

Cargo

We threw rocks at the crumpled freights. They'd jumped
the trestle, somersaulted into the creek.
The green cars had corroded to dark orange
and rotted. We threw in groups of ten, and you
were always nine to my six, seven, eight.
I threw hard, missed, threw harder, missed again,
while you just flipped a side-armed curve that arced

into the open doors so gracefully
it made me hate myself. The game, which had
somehow made itself up, collapsed. Set free,
we threw till dark, and when we stopped, the cars
were just about as empty as before —
for all your grace, for all my laboring.
We walked back to our run-down, rented house,

where we'd sit on the porch, drink gin, and read
the sides of cars as they rolled past. Sometimes
when cars had both doors open, we could glimpse
our neighbor's garden, and the man, his wife,
their little girl, weeding between the rows.
We saw it all the time, but seeing it
like that, through moving doors, made us despair

we'd ever have a garden. The self-pity of young men.
Awake, we almost kept it hidden. Past midnight,
the long, slow freights laden with grain slowed more
as they pulled through our neighborhood: earthquakes
a hundred feet or so from where we slept
in separate rooms — friends, poor, sharing a house
like brothers. That fierce! The slow trains shocked the ground.

The whole house trembled as they picked up speed.
But we grew used to them and dreamed intense,
competing dreams, as if we didn't know
the house still shook, the trains still lumbered past.
The cargo's gone — the milo, wheat, and corn
unloaded, delivered long ago. The grain
made into bread, the bread still on our tables.

New Headstones at the Shelby Springs Confederate Cemetery

Though wild, each flower has its name:
sweet william, dogtooth violet,
wild iris, wild geranium.
Some of the headstones, too, bear names:
Rucks, Murphry, Bookout. Mostly, though,
it's *Unknown Soldier CSA*.

It's late. At dusk, cool slanted light
glows opalescent on white stones,
and at the end of a long row
we stand and talk about — what else? —
mortality: unknown, a name,
unknown, me, you, and you.

                              I snap
a green weed from a grave and chew it
for its sharp, sour burst of juice.
One of you — which? — breaks off a stalk
and says, "Sheep sorrel."

                      It's *sorrel?* Sorrel!
She's dead and buried — and all my life
I'd heard my mother say *sheep sorrow*.
But now her teaching voice comes back
and says it slowly, properly
— *sheep sorrel* — so I will get it right.

But even she can't name these men
whose namelessness is now engraved
in marble. Adam had it easy.
He merely had to name the world's
ephemera, while we have to

remember it. Sheep sorrel, yes!
Wild iris, wood sage, chicory,
sweet william, Sarah, Norman, me,
and some red spiky thing, which blooms
at our feet as we walk back home.

Roberta was my mother's name.

The Unpromised Land

Montgomery, Alabama

Despite the noon sun shimmering on Court Street,
each day I leave my desk, and window-shop,
waste time, and use my whole lunch hour to stroll
the route the marchers took. The walk is blistering —
the kind of heat that might make you recall
Nat Turner skinned and rendered into grease
if you share my cheap liberal guilt for sins
before your time. I hold it dear. I know
if I had lived in 1861
I would have fought in butternut, not blue,
and never known I'd sinned. Nat Turner skinned
for doing what I like to think I'd do
if I were him.

                    Before the war
half-naked coffles were paraded to Court Square,
where Mary Chesnut gasped — "seasick" — to see
a bright mulatto on the auction block,
who bantered with the buyers, sang bawdy songs,
and flaunted her green satin dress, smart shoes.
I'm sure the poor thing knew who'd purchase her,
wrote Mrs. Chesnut, who plopped on a stool
to discipline her thoughts. Today I saw,
in that same square, three black girls pick loose tar,
flick it at one another's new white dresses,
then squeal with laughter. Three girls about the age
of those blown up in church in Birmingham.

The legendary buses rumble past the church
where Reverend King preached when he lived in town,
a town somehow more his than mine, despite
my memory of standing on Dexter Avenue

and watching, fascinated, a black man fry
six eggs on his Dodge Dart. Because I watched
he gave me one with flecks of dark blue paint
stuck on the yolk. My mother slapped my hand.
I dropped the egg. And when I tried to say
I'm sorry, Mother grabbed my wrist and marched me
back to our car.

                I can't hold to the present.
I've known these streets, their history, too long.
Two months before she died, my grandmother
remembered when I'd sassed her as a child,
and at the dinner table, in midbite,
leaned over, struck the grown man on the mouth.
And if I hadn't said *I'm sorry*, fast,
she would have gone for me again. My aunt,
from laughing, choked on a piece of lemon pie.
But I'm not sure. I'm just Christian enough
to think each sin taints every one of us,
a harsh philosophy that doesn't seem
to get me very far — just to the Capitol
each day at noon, my wet shirt clinging to my back.
Atop its pole, the stars-and-bars,
too heavy for the breeze, hangs listlessly.

Once, standing where Jeff Davis took his oath,
I saw the crippled governor wheeled into
the Capitol. He shrank into his chair,
so flaccid with paralysis he looked
like melting flesh, white as a maggot. He's fatter now.
He courts black votes, and life is calmer than
when Muslims shot whites on this street, and calmer

than when the Klan blew up Judge Johnson's house
or Martin Luther King's. My history could be worse.
I could be Birmingham. I could be Selma.
I could be Philadelphia, Mississippi.

Instead, I'm this small river town. Today,
as I worked at my desk, the boss
called to the janitor, *Jerome, I hear*
you get some lunchtime pussy every day.
Jerome, toothless and over seventy,
stuck the broom handle out between his legs:
Yessir! When the Big Hog talks
— he waggled the broomstick — *I gots to listen.*
He laughed. And from the corner of his eye,
he looked to see if we were laughing too.

Against Gardens

At first I'm careless with the hoe.
I spare curled delicate green weeds
and then the blue and purple buds,
the pretty ones. But soon enough,
locked in the measured savagery
of work, I choose the plants that give me
beans, eggplant, peas, cucumbers. I chop
geometry into green chaos.
And for a day or two it holds.
Rains come. The red earth shines. Weeds lunge
from under it as if the rain
had said a backwards prayer and called
them up by name: chickweed and clover,
wild onion, morning glory, dock.
I learn to hate them. One uncut root
spreads deep, sends up new shoots, returns
as that same plant I thought I'd killed.
And when I weed by hand, the leaves
tear free. Roots snap. The crisp white flesh
retreats a section at a time,
hiding the saving remnant from
my fingernails. The things we eat
don't grow so savagely. Each fruit
bears insect scars, rust, rot, and bruises.
We eat them and they ease my need
to find perfection in the world.
Tomatoes sampled by the birds
sag, drained. The insects riot. Blight
sets in. And soon the garden's theirs
more than it's mine. By August I give up,
sick of the work, sick even of the food,
which we have eaten meal after meal

until the kids protest and neighbors
won't take the gifts we offer them
to spare ourselves. Fall comes. And then,
relieved, I grab the garden fork
and turn the whole mess under. Although
I'm not prepared, myself, for spring,
the garden is — and I've relearned
how paradise becomes, each year,
both something gained and something given up.

Crucifixion

Montgomery, Alabama

In the hot dark they dug a hole —
quickly and with some panic dug
a small hole, tipped in the cross, braced it.
Flames surged through burlap soaked in kerosene.
A short lopsided, crude, half-burning cross.

Ah, Lord — each day, each breath, you're back
on some cross or another, nailed,
jabbed, taunted. And one eternal cross
burns through a hot night on this scorched
patch of suburban lawn. Judge Johnson's lawn.

I went to college with his son,
who, one fall day six months removed from Easter,
went in his room, shotgunned himself.

I would have said he died for us, our sins,
but I no longer know who Jesus is.
He's someone walking through his life — or hers —
until God whispers, *It's you*. And God's ignored.

Two boys — one fourteen and one fifteen —
heave their homemade cross onto a truck.
God's voice grows louder as the truck
turns down Christ's street. God's shouting now.
God roars. The boys ignite the cross, run off,
run hide, and wait to see whom God has chosen.

Or does God simply choose us all?

Prayer for an Ex-Wife

Outside, wind whips green limbs of willow, loud,
against my window. Bees struggle in midair,
land, cling to yellow catkins plumed with pollen.
They ride the whipcrack till they've done their work,
then stagger, laden, back into the air
and grab another brutal ride. I watch for hours,
doze off, then waken to a salmon moon.
I stretch, and suddenly remember how, asleep
but restless in her sleep, my first wife lashed
the bedsheets, moaned, and shuddered. I spread my hand
on her back, just below the shoulder blade.
She sweltered — damp, hot to the touch. *Dear God,*
I prayed, *let me bear all her suffering.*
Let me take it for her.
That was when I was very young, when I
thought suffering and work could do all things
or undo them. But now I pray, *God bless*
the willow, bless the bee, the wind, the pollen.
God bless the bedsheets and the salmon moon.

Christ as a Gardener

The boxwoods planted in the park spell LIVE.
I never noticed it until they died.
Before, the entwined green had smudged the word
unreadable. And when they take their own advice
again — come spring, come Easter — no one will know
a word is buried in the leaves. I love the way
that Mary thought her resurrected Lord
a gardener. It wasn't just the broad-brimmed hat
and muddy robe that fooled her: he was *that* changed.
He looks across the unturned field, the riot
of unscythed grass, the smattering of wildflowers.
Before he can stop himself, he's on his knees.
He roots up stubborn weeds, pinches the suckers,
deciding order here — what lives, what dies,
and how. But it goes deeper even than that.
His hands burn and his bare feet smolder. He longs
to lie down inside the long, dew-moist furrows
and press his pierced side and his broken forehead
into the dirt. But he's already done it —
passed through one death and out the other side.
He laughs. He kicks his bright spade in the earth
and turns it over. Spring flashes by, then harvest.
Beneath his feet, seeds dance into the air.
They rise, and he, not noticing, ascends
on midair steppingstones of dandelion,
of milkweed, thistle, cattail, and goldenrod.

Raking Out the Nest

The ladder tilted. I took a deep
slow breath, stood very still, then stomped —
and drove the taller leg, for balance,
into the rain-soaked earth. For weeks,
two mockingbirds had nested there,
under a loose board in my eaves.
For weeks, I'd wakened to jay shrieks,
crow calls, and something like a mad
electric pulse — *tchack! tchack!* — that drilled
into my nerves. For weeks, I'd dreamed
of my teeth breaking in my mouth.
Now, barefoot, poised on the top rung,
I groped above my head, raked out
gray, ashy clumps of dung, twigs, feathers —
and four blue eggs speckled with brown.
Wind blew the light trash back. It drifted
down my shirt collar, stuck in my hair.
Wings blasted near my face. I flinched.
The ladder shifted and I wondered,
absurdly, if I would miss the birds'
crazed voices howling through my house,
like ghosts. I nailed the loose board shut
and smacked it with my palm. It boomed.
I eased down off the tilted ladder.
The clean house settled into silence.

The Garden Changes

When I was young, I grew
dull plants returning food
for work. But I, now older,
repent my practicality.
I've renounced beans, and turned
to crocus, gladiola,
and coreopsis. I've moved
past zinnia, marigold,
to bougainvillea.
I've even learned to love
poor salvia, which blooms
on August days, when few flowers
will venture anything
but green. The summer's short
and ornament is what
I want — all vividness.
Not pasty cauliflower
and not potatoes, whose
gnarled flesh is more and more
like mine. Give me bright blossoms
against the teeming green.
Give me orange flags, blue horns,
white faces, yellow wings.
Give me the purple throat,
breathless, of calla lilies —
and red, red, red, red, red.

Communion in the Asylum

We kneel. Some of us kneel better than others
and do not have to clutch the rail or sway
against those next to us. We hold up hands
to take the body in, and some of our hands
— a few — are firmer than the others. They
don't tremble, don't have to be held in the priest's
encircling hands and guided to our lips.
And some of us can hold the wafer, all of it,
inside our mouths. And when the careful priest
tips wine across our lips, many of us, for reverence,
don't moan or lurch or sing songs to ourselves.
But we all await the grace that's promised us.

Psalm Against Psalms

Unto the pure all things are pure.

God had Isaiah eat hot coals,
Ezekiel eat shit, and they sang
his praises. I've eaten neither, despite
my childhood need to test most things
inside my mouth. My brothers and I
would pop small frogs over our lips.
They'd crouch in the close dark, then bump,
tickling, against the roofs of our mouths.
We'd brace, try not to laugh, because
the winner was the one who last
spit out his frog. Actually,
it's not my story. It happened
to a woman who told it to me
right after I leaned over, kissed her.
But I think it is my memory
because I wish it were — as I
have thought of shit and fire and what
they'd taste like in my mouth. Kids jam the world,
hand over fist, into their mouths,
but fire only once, shit only once.
And even pregnant women, who,
where I come from, will eat red clay,
not knowing they eat it for the iron,
just knowing something drives them out
into the fields to eat earth — secret,
furtive, ashamed — do not eat fire.
Smokers smoke, pulling the fire closer
and closer to their lips, but no one,
except by accident, pulls it

into his mouth. A few professionals
pretend to eat the blossom off a torch,
and then exhale a violent billowing,
like a soul blasting from the flesh
that cannot hold it. And I have even heard
of a man, who, in a darkened kitchen,
turned all the burners on and watched
orange spirals floating in the dark,
shimmering like elaborate UFOs. He watched
until he couldn't hold back any longer;
and he climbed on the counter, pressed
his naked chest against the spirals
as if he could embrace the fire, love it,
consume the burning, and not be burnt.

Isaiah ate the blood-red ember.
Ezekiel ate the dung. It went in fire
and came out praise. It went in shit
and came praise from his mouth. And this
is where I stick. I pray: thank, ask,
confess. But praise — dear God! — it clings
like something dirty on my tongue,
like shit. Or burns because it is a lie.
And yet I try: I pray and ask
for praise, then force the balking words
out of my mouth as if the saying them
could form the glowing coal — cool,
smooth as a ruby — on my tongue.
Or mold inside my mouth the shit
that melts like caramel — and thereby,
by magic, change my heart. Instead
I croak the harsh begrudging praise

of those who conjure grace, afraid
that it might come, afraid it won't.
But if grace tore through me and spoke,
as God in his strange redundant way
put on my tongue to praise himself,
I'd hear the words I said and learn
why I invented all the horrors of the world,
learn why I made us humans love
our hard sweet lives, then added death
to give it all intensity.

When she dropped food, my mother scooped
it from the floor, flicked off the grit,
blew on it, and pronounced it clean
before she put it on my plate.
I do the same. And when I cut my hand,
I jam the finger in my mouth
and suck my own blood, hot and salty
as melted butter. I'm not fastidious
between extremes of fire and shit — the one
so pure it smolders on our flesh,
the other one so pure our flesh
refuses it, expels it, walks away.
That's why so few of us are prophets.
God-like, they feast on purities,
pure spirit or pure excrement.
I'm smaller, human, in between,
a leavening of dirt with fire.
and I must be, with every passing day,
more careful of what goes into my mouth,
more reckless of what issues forth.